THE NEST'S DARK EYE

poems by

Dianne Stepp

Finishing Line Press
Georgetown, Kentucky

THE NEST'S DARK EYE

Copyright © 2022 by Dianne Stepp
ISBN 978-1-64662-967-1 First Edition
All rights reserved under International and Pan-American Copyright Conventions. No part of this book may be reproduced in any manner whatsoever without written permission from the publisher, except in the case of brief quotations embodied in critical articles and reviews.

ACKNOWLEDGMENTS

Grateful acknowledgement is made to the following journals or presses for first publishing these poems, or earlier versions of them:

Half-Moon of Clay: "The time you want to speak of" and "Estate Sale"
Sweet Mercies: "Grief"
Tar River Poetry: After We Binge-Watch
Windfall Press: "Bill Jake Hollow"
Comstock Review: "Annual Yield"

Publisher: Leah Huete de Maines
Editor: Christen Kincaid
Cover Art: Barbara Sanders
Author Photo: Sam Blair
Cover Design: Elizabeth Maines McCleavy

Order online: www.finishinglinepress.com
also available on amazon.com

Author inquiries and mail orders:
Finishing Line Press
PO Box 1626
Georgetown, Kentucky 40324
USA

Table of Contents

Afterwards 1

Aubade 3

The time you want to speak of 4

Annual Yield 6

History 7

Abundance 8

Estate Sale 9

At the Steam Up 10

Metaphor 12

Lament 13

Matins 14

Mike and I Drive the Hana Highway Again After Your Death 15

After We Binge-Watch 16

Grief 17

Solace 19

That Last Summer 20

Bill Jake Hollow 21

It Could Have Been Anywhere 22

for David

Afterwards

> —*It was as though a bulldozer shoved relentlessly at the bricks of his life, as we tried to shore up the crumbling mortar.*

Beneath the shade of the junipers,
beyond the wildflowers
tangled in the heads of ripe grass,
a deer swivels her ears
toward the sound of my voice
over the camp stove. And later,
after you dry the last dish
and I set my camp chair in the shade,
a breeze sweeps down the canyon
with a sound like the ocean,
or the rush of a distant train.
The heads of the grasses nod.
And now the doe steps delicately,
intent on her browse
under the boughs of the trees.
She twitches her tail. Her ears
flick against the flies
as she spreads her legs,
squats like a woman
taking a long, satisfying pee.

On our trek next day,
we stop to gulp the shade
of every juniper on the way
to the ranch where three brothers
raised mules for saddle
in the First World War. Washouts
from last spring's floods corrugate
the trail. A mountain bluebird
perches on a fencepost, a brazen bit
of male fluff who scolds from post
to branch. We cross the bridge,

look down at the lush meadow
of unbelievably green grass
where the solo cabin one brother
built for himself still stands.
I lean for a moment
against you, and ask
if you think my son
might have found solace here
in this thigh-deep beauty
hugged between basalt cliffs.
In this cabin, scarred
by scores of winters, squared off,
log-butted against the wind.

Aubade

As I drift toward the rim
of dawn from the warm
nest our bodies make, I hear
from the woods behind our house
the soft hoots of an owl,
and quiet my breath to tune
to the pulse of what remains
of the night, straining to listen
for the call to repeat. Yes,
yes, the same distant notes
float again from the firs.
And then, from the further
distance, an echo,
faint, barely audible. Again
the call, again the response.
And now I sense you listening too,
both of us concentrating—
your finger, a soft tap
on my shoulder,
parsing the phrasing,
both of us trying to hold
the sounds inside ourselves
before they slip away.

The time you want to speak of

is a town you haven't visited in years,
signposts torn down, only the river
to guide you, and an old covered bridge

linking now with then, and on the farther side
someone's house you have to walk behind
to find the lane, and the rose

that climbs high into the pine, turns
its face toward the midnight sky.
The old brick steps lead to the front door

that opens now at your slightest touch.
The hallway, the blue rug,
the phone swinging on its cord.

And you on your knees
in your nightdress, your boy
on his back on the floor. Your hands

pushing on his chest. And a voice
that comes from the far white corners
says *one and two and three and four*

and breathe and one and two and
now the firemen rush through the front door,
they put a mask over your boy's nose,

clappers on his chest and say kindly
a little faster now one two three four five,
giving you that, your hands

pushing down on his small bare chest,
blue pajamas pulled aside, the little animal
of his life coming back, yes back. Now

they adjust the oxygen mask over his face,
and you watch that young woman you were,
all the flowers on her night dress trembling

as they lift your boy to the stretcher,
carry him out, and you wish
she could hear your voice,

that you could touch her shoulder
across the years, whisper
Thank you for the arms

that gathered the small rigid body
from the bed,
for the phone call, the dash

down the hall to unlatch the front door.
You watch her pull on her blue jeans,
climb into the ambulance,

hunch over your boy. Red lights
strobe the frightened face
that, unseeing, stares out at you.

Annual Yield
for Mike

When you write the check
for the taxes on the extra lot
behind our house, I say

we could be adding zeros
to our bank account by selling that lot
instead of growing garlic.

We could be putting our feet up
instead of toting bundles to dry
in the breezeway each summer.

We ink the name of each variety
on a small white tag—
Metechi, Korean Red, China Stripe—

musing the route each traveled
to find us. Instead
we could fly to Marrakech

like our kids, prowl the bazaar
behind the hotel for brass tapers
to warm our table. In August

we trim the bulbs, papery
with transparent skins,
reserve the biggest for seed.

October we're on our knees
in mud. Each pearly clove
six inches apart, six deep.

January, first leaves push
through snow. Scapes
curl in May. July,

we grab the spade, wedge it deep.
Is this what love is?
Each corm a knot of oily fire.

History

Today, on the 75th anniversary
        of the liberation of Auschwitz,
I sit in my favorite coffee shop
spreading cream cheese on half a bagel,

taking stock of where in our house
        we could build a room
to hide someone–a fake wall
in the attic, camouflage of old nails,

used wood. Or in the crawl space
        under the kitchen floor,
through the narrow passage in the closet
blocked with shoes. Four taps

beside the stove would signal
        danger. Two, all clear.
Each night we'd relay the bucket
to the toilet, trying not to spill.

In a cabinet I keep my mother's
        war-time figurines: Bambi,
Flower, the skunk, Mickey. An entire flock
of unnamed porcelain birds.

In the camps a casual hand
        gestures right
or left. As I sip
my mug of coffee.

As I suck the slice of orange
garnishing my plate.

Abundance
--Skagit Valley, 1965

They picked pholiotas, chanterelles,
stewed them in butter,
kneaded cardamom, salt
into good brown bread,
hiked logging roads for huckleberries,
parting the glittering leaves
to pluck the ruby fruit.
From the farmer down the road
they bought their milk for pennies,
churned butter, ice cream. At the sink
brewed dandelion wine
from hundreds of cow-pasture suns,
morphed them to bottled
moonlight. They drove the shore
to the reservation where the Swinomish
beach-seined salmon, carried home
silver flanks to sweeten on alder fires.
Who, oh who, could blame them
for thinking they would never die.

Estate Sale

It was winter, and though midday,
the lights inside the house were on.
You headed up the walk while I
stayed outside to admire the fig trees
which had grown so abundantly
in the orchards of my youth
I forgot I loved them.

Through the window I saw the tassel of your cap
moving above other heads bent over boxes
that held the stuff of other people's lives.
A row of drinking glasses glittered yellow
inside the pane, and someone held up a pair
of black boots trimmed with fur.

I'd forgotten how fast daylight fades,
already the crows were gathering,
flapping like black rags
over the roofs of neighboring houses
into the bare canopy of the maple
towering behind the garage, their voices
a hoarse chorus, rising, falling back again.

Like a river whirled to crest, the wind
snatched at my coat and gloves. I felt
there must be a key hidden in plain sight, a key
to unlock the meaning of everything.

Some of the people started to leave.
One carried a lamp, another
a chintz-covered chair, two people
a desk, a box of drinking glasses.
I don't remember what you carried out.
I remember only the tassel of your cap,
the rusted baubles of last year's figs,
and the crows, whirling,
flapping down the guttering sky,
legs outstretched, braced for landing.

At the Steam Up
Donald, Oregon

It was years ago,
wandering the display of machines
from another era—
threshers, tillers, grinders, tractors,
all belching clouds of steam,
hiccupping, coughing, purring
under the August sun.

And in the fields of dried grass
stood tables of old tools:
pliers, vises, wedges,
mysterious collars, cogs, bolts,
some tools so old no one
could remember their use.

Among these I found a small
black-and-white photograph
with pinked edges,
cracked, curled with age.

Sprawled on a bench,
a skeletal corpse, eyes open,
limbs contorted in agony of rigor.

And to the side, on a stoop,
two women stare at the camera,
eyes dull with starvation.

I felt the shock of questions.
Where? Who? A GI with a Kodak
in the Second World War?
Leningrad? Greece?

How did it come to be here?

I hid the photo in my palm
as I thought what to do.
Should I carry it off, take it home
to a kinder rest. Bury it? Burn it?

Why did I put it back and walk away?

Metaphor

I invent an equation
for metaphor
wherein *x* is *unknown*
and *b* is the noun *despair*
and plus or minus is *real*
whereas *square root*
is the inverse of *house*
times *c* which equals
empty.

Do you see what I mean?

And *a* is of *course absence*
whereas *-b squared*
is *despair* doubled
and *square root* morphs
to *nightmare.*
So *despair*
is an *empty house*
which is multiplied by four
and divided by two times
absence.

Am I making sense?

And the walls are papered
with *voices*
which solves for *x*
which is a man
coming *unraveled.*
And the equal sign alters to *razors*
slashing both ways.
And the black paint
the tub
the blood.

Did I say that?

Lament

When he was alive I grieved
at how he used to scold me
because I whacked the blade
of the chopping knife

on the side of a clove
of garlic. At how he rolled
his eyes when I salted
my eggs, or jutted his jaw

at some remark I made.
Revenge of the son grown,
I said to myself, ruing
my own rebukes to my mother.

I fix the clove on the board
to prepare the stew for dinner,
and feel the deep tears rise.
Oh, my darling son,

how could you leave us so?

Matins

Mornings I cross the wet grass
to the greenhouse
to see the tomato seedlings.
I check the temperature,
admire their resilience,
these ferny beings,
stems as thick as my finger
despite the cold,
or perhaps because of it.

Though I miss their little pots
on my bedroom desk.
Miss opening the curtain
for them each morning.
Miss the weeks I fed
and watered them,
fretting their spindly growth
in weak indoor light.

And though I rarely pray,
not down on my knees
sort of prayer,
it was devotion I felt
all those days
I leaned over them
in gratitude
for each small leaf
that trembled.

Mike and I Drive the Hana Highway Again After Your Death

Every hill we pass
choked with bamboo,
every racing, white-frothed
gulley, every crimson bloom
fluttering in the canopy
like a rare bird
reminds me of the sweet
bitter song
of better years:

Rain caught in seven
crystal fists at Seven Pools.
The boardwalk through yellow,
clacking bamboo.
Your wife holding a split guava
to show the pink
cup of seeds:

"Such a tremendous life-force," she said,
"See how like a little womb."

The frog-lilt
of your baby son—*ribbet, ribbet*—
his arms around my neck
as we drove.

After We Binge-Watch

the police drama in which the image
of the daughter who hanged herself
flashes repeatedly on the screen
of her mother's memory,
Mike tells me he wants to throw
his body across mine, plug my ears,
shield my eyes, yank out
the television cord. But I tell him
I feel absolutely nothing—
the swollen face and staring eyes
unable to tip me from the rock
of my grief, and I don't know why.
Although I don't explain,
not yet, not yet, the times early
or late in bed, how the lens
of imagination clicks in quick
shudders: the yellow electric cord,
the ceiling beam barely high enough,
the clear plastic he spread below.
Four days in the heat of the jungle
in Hana. The deck door, was it open?
The screen on the window, was it
gnawed by rodents? The ripped
arm of the sofa, was it so close
he could have changed his mind?
How long, dear god, how long?

Grief

Every day I walk fence,
tracing an invisible line.
I shift my weight.
One foot to the other.
Turn my head, always to the left,
never the right,
peering into the dusk
of that other world
where he paces—tall, thin, pale—
beside me, but facing
the opposite direction.

I've hurt myself.
Pulled a muscle at waistline on my right side,
craning to see, twisting
to search the shape
of his death.
I stretch to ease the pain.
I sit down. I put my right leg
across my left knee.
I lean forward. I feel
the pull in my thigh.

Someone has imposed a screen
along the border between us.
A no man's land where all color
is subtracted.

When I turn my head
he stands in a night that never
falls. His face ashen
above faded denim.
Is it accusing,
stunned, or merely blank?

My own face is a mask.
It stares at me from the mirror.
In the morning I scrub it
with a soapy cloth. Rub cream
into it, around the eyes,
forehead, cheeks.
I apply gloss to its lips.

If I want to, I can make it smile.

Solace

If I weren't a city girl
I'd get myself a Jersey cow
with a good temper
who'd walk to the barn
of her own accord
and wait for me at
the milking parlor.
And not kick
or flick her tail
in my face
or let down
until I was ready.
Let the magpies
of progress screech.
I'd still submit
my days to mirror
the needs of her body.
Mornings and evenings
I'd soap the swell
of her udder. I'd lean
into the warm brew of her flank
and it would be like leaning
against the side of a mountain.

That Last Summer

The clematis hadn't overgrown
the corner post of the deck yet,
hadn't sent its urgent vines
along the roof-beam. Robins
hadn't sought safety
in its shadows. Their chicks'
yellow beaks hadn't opened
like twin flowers on wobbly stems.
I hadn't watched from my deck chair
the parent birds fly relays,
worms bristling
from their beaks, hadn't peeked
at the blue fragment
in the nest's dark eye.

Wild rabbits
hadn't found our yard yet.
My fingers hadn't twitched
to touch the soft fur
of the kits hidden
in a twist of garden mulch.
The sun hadn't shone
through the sheer membrane
of the mother's ear,
staining it red.

I hadn't learned
to grow garlic yet,
hadn't learned to braid
their stalks,
never got the chance to send
the perfume of their oils
home with you.
Oh, my son,
why couldn't I find a way
to keep you tethered to us?

Bill Jake Hollow

You come to a place like this
to find refuge from your life
in the city. No traffic, no people,
no internet. Only the contrail
of a lone plane overhead. At noon
night hawks pierce the sky
for insects. Beyond the flats
erosion creases the brown hills.
A sparse forest of junipers
tries to hold the soil from its desire
to slide. From the hollow
wind comes up
blusters a bit, slackens.
Just a few white clouds—
slow moving boats in a tranquil sea.
You come to a place like this
as to a pool, to restore yourself
in the desert landscape. To swim
slowly. Breast stroke, side stroke,
to float peacefully on your back.
You come to walk across the flats
to the river, to step carefully
through a whole village
of pink flowers.

It Could Have Been Anywhere

But it was the Belle Surf Café in Kihei
where I sipped coffee

and watched the merchants raise the shutters
on their open-air shops.

Beneath chairs on the patio little zebra doves
cooed and scrabbled for crumbs.

The tall palms leaned in.
I was still desperate for answers.

What I did or didn't do?
How far back before all the forks in the road

disappeared, and one road only
led to the cabin in Hana

where my oldest son took his life.
Took his life. This is the language I used

to soften the truth of what he did to himself.
From the depths of her shop

a woman selling sarongs carried armfuls
of purple, red, turquoise sashes,

arranged them on hangers,
and selecting one with white magnolias

splashed across a sea of black
she draped it on a silver rack where it flew solo.

Dianne Stepp's poems have appeared in a variety of literary journals and anthologies, including *High Desert Journal, Cider Press Review, Tar River Poetry, Sugar House Review, Comstock Review* and others. She is a recipient of an Oregon Literary Arts Fellowship and writers' residencies at Caldera and Playa. Her chapbooks *Half-Moon of Clay* and *Sweet Mercies* were published by Finishing Line Press in 2006 and 2017 respectively. She is a graduate of the Warren Wilson MFA Program in Poetry, and is also a tapestry artist, spinner, teacher and avid gardener. A retired counselor, she lives in Portland, Oregon with her husband.

www.ingramcontent.com/pod-product-compliance
Lightning Source LLC
LaVergne TN
LVHW041522070426
835507LV00012B/1763